AF407091

Hey, hi!

Thank you for trusting us with your story time. We certainly hope you enjoy the story ahead! A few quick reminders before you begin-

 Be sure to flip to the back for some fun facts (some might say the funnest), to learn more about our bud Mungo and to meet the author and illustrator!

 **Hey, Hi!** Books are books that give. A portion of proceeds from every book sold goes toward helping others! Proceeds from this book will go toward the education of children in need. We greatly appreciate your support.

 Be sure to visit our website at **heyhimediallc.com** for more!

Dedication:
This book is dedicated to my grandmother Sylvia H. Duncan.
-In loving memory of our history trips and wonderful conversations. -
I love you very much.

ON YOUR HORSE, MR. REVERE!

Written by Scott Watkins

Illustrated by Casey Pipetti

Hey, Hi!

A Family Media Company

One if by land, two if by sea.

The whole world stood still as Revere made his decree.

Fast like a bolt, voice full of intention!
He galloped through town.

The British he did mention.

Far in distance not in spirit,
our future leader stands by.

Washington knew it'd begun at the horseman's decry.

A land full of hope.
A nation ready to win.

To fight or surrender, both considered a sin.

Farmers and merchants standing side by side.

With butchers and fur traders; all ready to die.

For to fight such a tyrant is to
be considered treason.

But to live without freedom is to live
without reason.

On this night a voice is heard,
it serves as a warning...

...for tomorrow a single shot will ring out
in the morning.

And so, breathe it in Mr. Washington,
the calm of this night.

For very soon my good sir,
you're in for a fight.

The Funnest of Facts!

① Paul Revere Was Part of a Team

Paul Revere was one of many colonists who formed a team to alert others to the whereabouts of the British Army or "Regulars" as they called them in those days. On April 18th, 1775, Dr. Joseph Warren heard of the British plan and tasked Paul Revere, William Dawes, and Samuel Prescott to ride out and warn others that the British Army was coming and heading for Lexington and Concord in Massachusetts.

② George Washington Was Not General Washington Yet

The battles of Lexington and Concord are considered the first of the American Revolution. However, at this time, many colonists were hoping to avoid a war. In fact, the Continental Army had not even been formed yet. Two months after the battles, the Continental Army was formed and George Washington was named general June 19, 1775.

③ Paul Revere Was Arrested During His Ride!

Yes, you read that correctly. Before reaching their destination, Paul Revere, William Dawes, and Samuel Prescott were spotted by some British troops. Mr. Dawes and Mr. Prescott got away but Mr. Revere was captured and questioned. Don't worry though, he was released not long after. Thankfully, their message reached enough people who were able to warn the towns and two important founding fathers who were in Lexington- John Hancock and Samuel Adams.

Meet Mungo!

Did you notice our tiny revolutionary, Mungo?

Mungo will be joining us for all our history adventures!

Guess what?

Mungo was an actual squirrel from revolutionary times! Squirrels were very popular pets in those days. One of the biggest squirrel fans was Benjamin Franklin! He actually gifted Mungo to a young girl while he was living in England as a diplomat.

About the Author & Illustrator

Don't let the beard, tattoos, general adult responsibilities or age fool you. Scott is a large child at heart. Scott's love for storytelling began at a young age and has grown into a mission to impact and enrich the lives of others through fun and meaningful stories.

Although Scott is not a #1 Bestselling New York Times Author, his wonderful wife and mother say he's a #1 best seller in their eyes. Scott calls a little town outside of Pittsburgh, PA home with his wife and darling daughter. When not writing, Scott loves preaching, learning, sports and anything outdoors (or as they'd say in the old days "out of doors").

 @ heyhimedia    heyhimediallc.com

Casey has been drawing since she could hold a pencil - and she never stopped. Most days you can find her diligently toiling away over her Wacom tablet in her home office. She is inspired by cute and colorful things, animals, vintage illustrations, and contemporary art.

Despite her colorful and whimsical style, she really enjoys spooky things and rainy days. Born in Hollidaysburg, PA and a resident of Pittsburgh for a half-decade, she is happy to call Pennsylvania her home. When she isn't working (which is rare) she is gaming, playing guitar, walking her golden retriever, or fueling her curiosity about life by reading and studying various topics.

 @ happygoatdraws    happygoatdraws.com